Welcome to Our World

SECOND EDITION

Series Editors
Joan Kang Shin & JoAnn (Jodi) Crandall

Authors
Jill Korey O'Sullivan & Joan Kang Shin

NATIONAL GEOGRAPHIC
LEARNING

T0288699

Australia • Brazil • Canada • Mexico • Singapore • United Kingdom • United States

Scope and Sequence

Let's Share! p. 4

Express Needs, Apologies,
Make Suggestions,
Give Compliments
Song: I Need The Blue Paint

Language in Use: I need the paint. I need the paint, too.   Let's share! OK!
I'm sorry! That's OK.   I like your picture! Thanks. I like your picture, too!

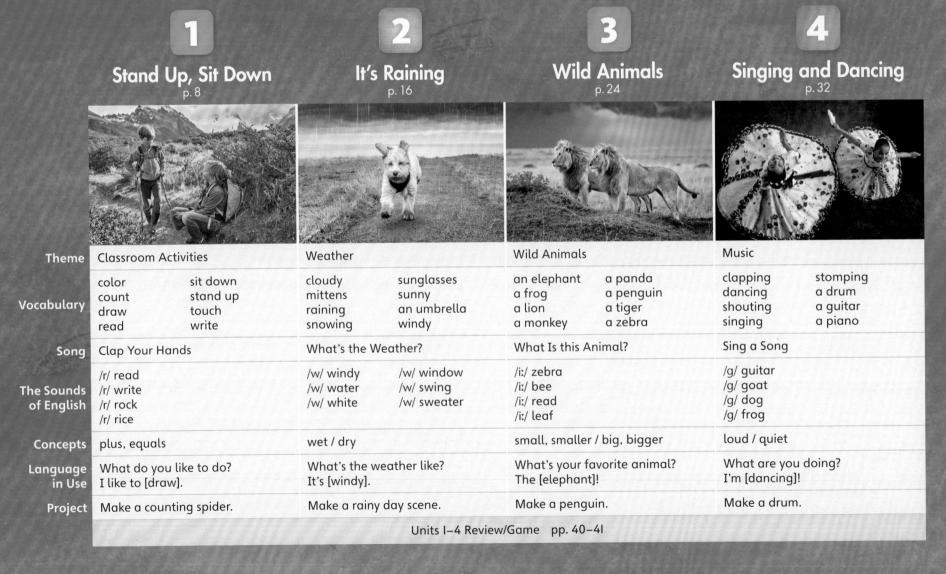

	1 Stand Up, Sit Down p. 8	**2** It's Raining p. 16	**3** Wild Animals p. 24	**4** Singing and Dancing p. 32
Theme	Classroom Activities	Weather	Wild Animals	Music
Vocabulary	color sit down count stand up draw touch read write	cloudy sunglasses mittens sunny raining an umbrella snowing windy	an elephant a panda a frog a penguin a lion a tiger a monkey a zebra	clapping stomping dancing a drum shouting a guitar singing a piano
Song	Clap Your Hands	What's the Weather?	What Is this Animal?	Sing a Song
The Sounds of English	/r/ read /r/ write /r/ rock /r/ rice	/w/ windy /w/ window /w/ water /w/ swing /w/ white /w/ sweater	/iː/ zebra /iː/ bee /iː/ read /iː/ leaf	/g/ guitar /g/ goat /g/ dog /g/ frog
Concepts	plus, equals	wet / dry	small, smaller / big, bigger	loud / quiet
Language in Use	What do you like to do? I like to [draw].	What's the weather like? It's [windy].	What's your favorite animal? The [elephant]!	What are you doing? I'm [dancing]!
Project	Make a counting spider.	Make a rainy day scene.	Make a penguin.	Make a drum.

Units 1–4 Review/Game   pp. 40–41

Welcome to Our World 3

SECOND EDITION

	5 **See, Smell, Hear** p. 42	**6** **Story Time** p. 50	**7** **It's a Party!** p. 58	**8** **Our World** p. 66

Theme	The Senses	Stories	Parties	The World
Vocabulary	drink see eat smell feel taste hear	a castle a knight a dragon a princess a giant a queen a king a treasure	a balloon ice cream a cake pizza candles a present candy	a bridge a river a cloud a road a mountain the sky the ocean
Song	Oh, What Do You See?	In a Castle	It's a Party	Where Are You Going, Friend?
The Sounds of English	/eɪ/ taste /eɪ/ table /eɪ/ eight /eɪ/ play	/dʒ/ giant /dʒ/ juice /dʒ/ jump	/uː/ balloon /uː/ boots /uː/ shoes /uː/ blue	/oʊ/ road /oʊ/ goat /oʊ/ nose /oʊ/ piano
Concepts	hard / soft	beginning, middle, end	more / less	the world, a country, a city
Language in Use	What do you [see]? I [see] [a crayon].	What's the story about? It's about [a king] and [a dragon].	Would you like some [ice cream]? Yes, please. / No, thanks.	Where do you live? I live in [India].
Project	Make a five senses poster.	Make a dragon.	Make a pizza.	Make a globe.

Units 5–8 Review/Game   pp. 74–75

Let's Share!

Look and listen. Say. TR: 0.1

1 Stand Up, Sit Down

Listen, point, and say. TR: 1.1

Listen and say. TR: 1.2

stand up

Boys taking a break from
hiking, Patagonia, Argentina

sit down

VOCABULARY   Listen, point, and say. TR: 1.3

touch

read

count

write

draw

color

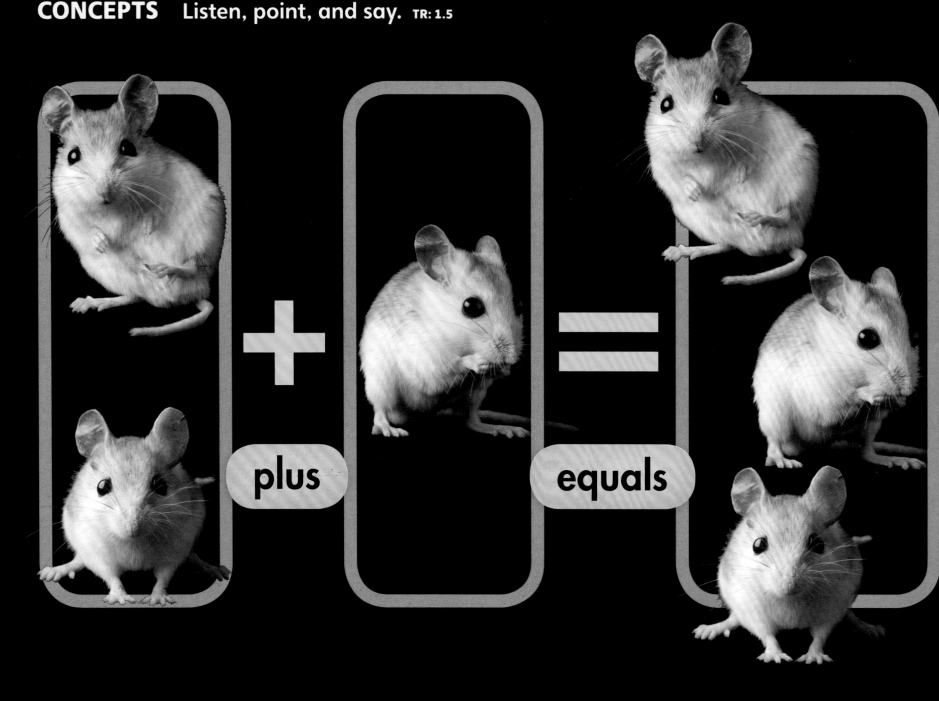

plus

equals

PRACTICE Say and stick.

PROJECT   Make a counting spider.

2 It's Raining

Listen, point, and say. TR: 2.1

Listen and say. TR: 2.2

A cockapoo running
in the rain in the UK

an umbrella

raining

windy

cloudy

sunglasses

sunny

mittens

snowing

PRACTICE Draw lines and say the words.

wet

dry

A tiger in Malaysia

A tiger in India

A park in Russia

A nature reserve in Belgium

PROJECT Make a rainy day scene.

3 Wild Animals

Listen, point, and say. TR: 3.1

Listen and say. TR: 3.2

Two lions in Kenya

24

a frog

a penguin

a zebra

a lion

an elephant

a tiger

a monkey

a panda

PRACTICE   Draw a line and say the word.

small

smaller

African elephants in Kenya

bigger

big

PROJECT   Make a penguin.

4 Singing and Dancing

Listen, point, and say. TR: 4.1

Listen and say. TR: 4.2

Dancers in Chile

singing

clapping

stomping

a drum

a guitar

dancing

shouting

a piano

PRACTICE   Count and connect. Say the words.

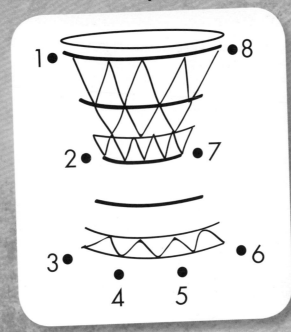

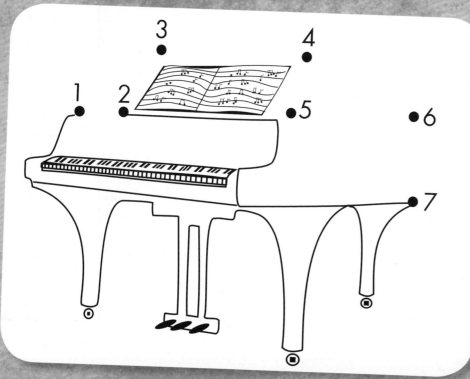

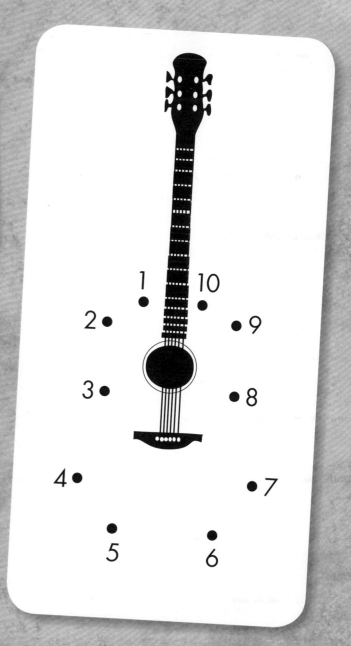

loud

quiet

Children playing
trumpets, India

A girl playing an
instrument, Chile

PRACTICE Match, stick, and say.

PROJECT Make a drum.

REVIEW Listen and circle. TR: 4.7

5 See, Smell, Hear

Listen, point, and say. TR: 5.1

Listen and say. TR: 5.2

A red fox and
a butterfly

VOCABULARY   Listen, point, and say.   TR: 5.3

see

smell

feel

eat

hear

taste

drink

PRACTICE Circle and say the words.

hard

soft

A statue of a bear in Finland

A teddy bear

PROJECT Make a five senses poster.

6 Story Time

Listen, point, and say. TR: 6.1

Listen and say. TR: 6.2

a castle

Schloss Neuschwanstein Castle in Germany

a king

a queen

a princess

a knight

a treasure   a dragon

a giant

beginning

middle

end

PRACTICE   Stick and say.

PROJECT   Make a dragon.

7 It's a Party!

A giant panda and
two birthday cakes

58

candles

a cake

ice cream

a balloon

pizza

a present

candy

PRACTICE   Circle and say the words.

more

less

PRACTICE Point and say.

Would you like some ice cream?

Yes, please.

No, thanks.

PROJECT   Make a pizza.

8 Our World

Listen, point, and say. TR: 8.1

Listen and say. TR: 8.2

Mountains in the
Guilin region of China

a cloud

a mountain

a bridge

the sky

the ocean

a river

a road

PRACTICE Draw and say the words.

SONG Listen and sing. TR: 8.4

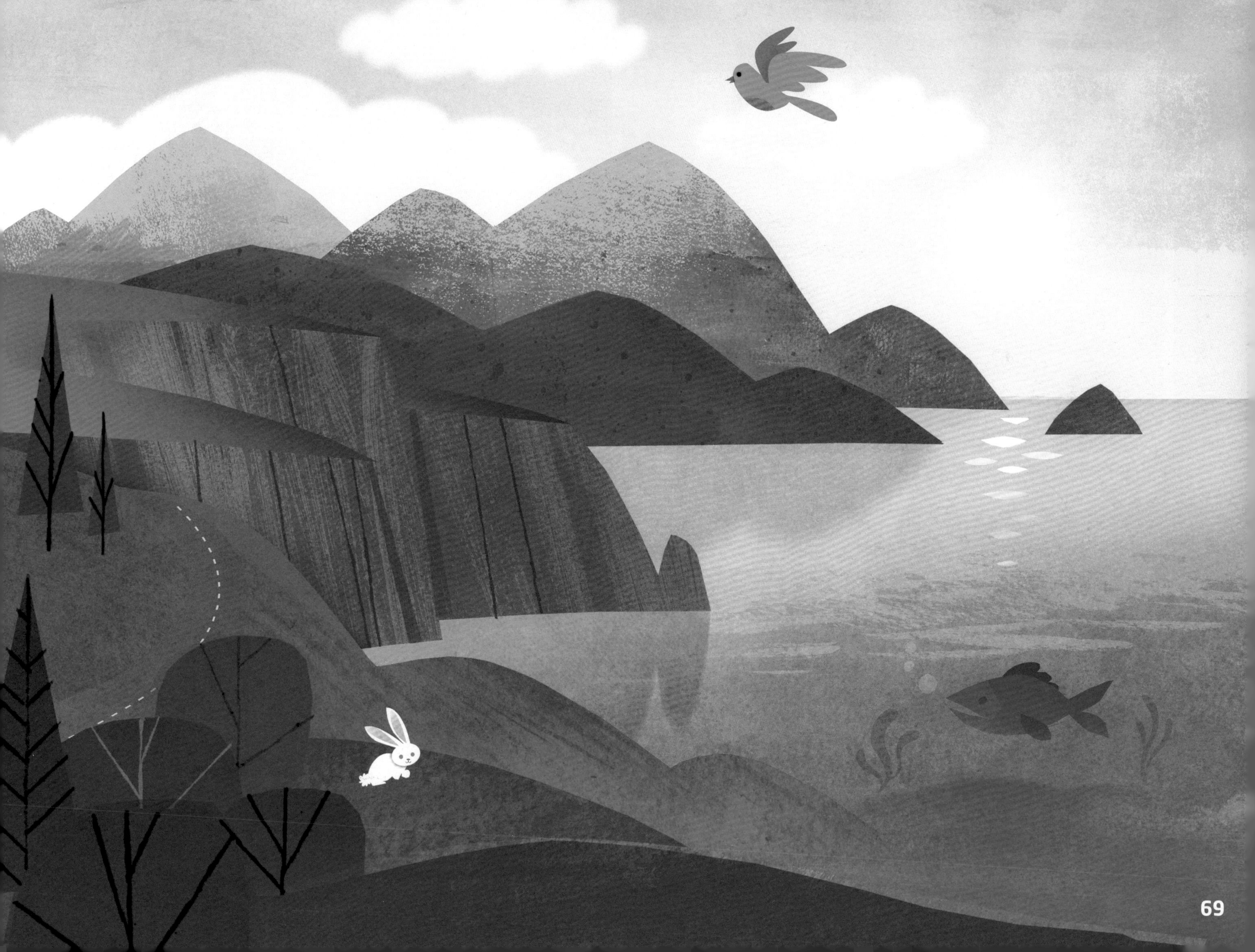

a country

Mexico

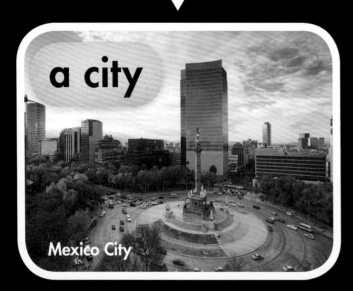

a city

Mexico City

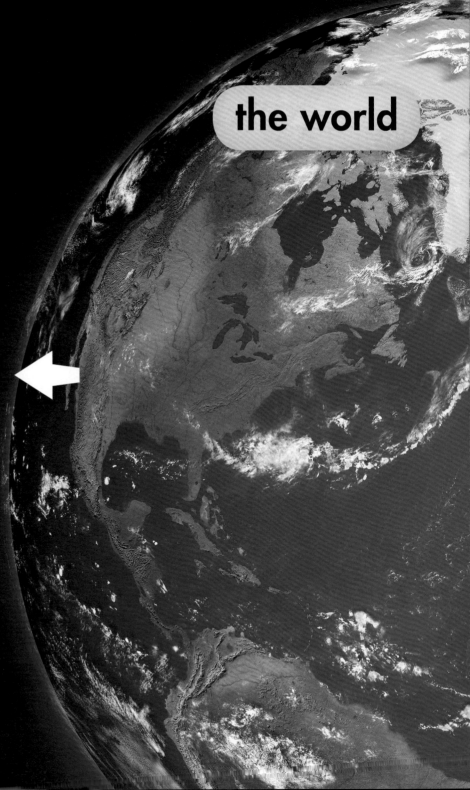

the world

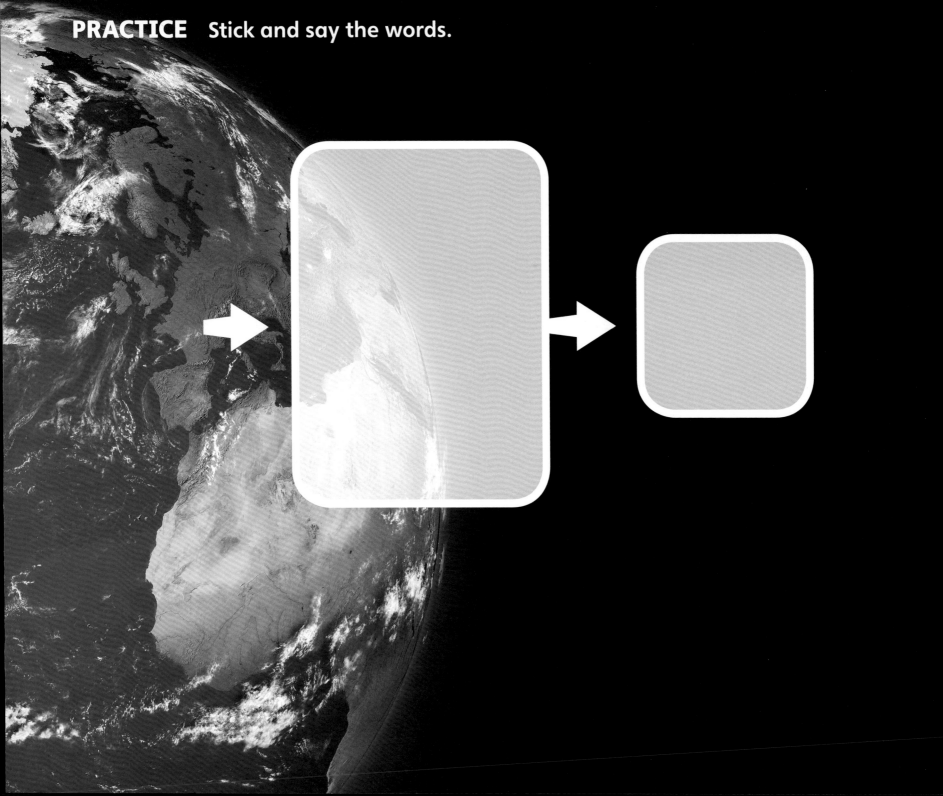

LANGUAGE IN USE   Color. Listen, point, and say.   TR: 8.6

PROJECT   Make a globe.

GAME Play and say.

75

The Alphabet TR: A–Z

A apple

B bird

C cat

D dog

I insect

J juice

K king

L lion

Q queen

R rabbit

S socks

T train

U umbrella

E egg

F fire truck

G goat

H hand

M milk

N nose

O orange

P puzzle

V violin

W window

X box

Y yogurt

Z zebra

I Can...

1 I can talk about things I do in class.

2 I can talk about the weather.

3 I can talk about wild animals.

4 I can talk about music.

5 I can talk about the senses.

6 I can talk about stories.

7 I can talk about parties.

8 I can talk about my world.

Chant and Song Lyrics

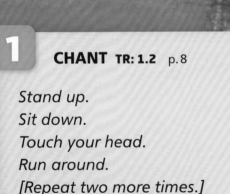

SONG TR: 0.5 p.7
I Need the Blue Paint

I need, I need the blue paint.
I need, I need the blue paint, too!
Oh! We both need the blue paint.
Let's share the blue paint,
my friend.

1

SONG TR: 1.4 p.11
Clap Your Hands

Clap your hands.   *Clap your hands.*
It's time for school.   *It's time for school.*
It's time to read and color, too.   *It's time to write and color, too.*
It's time to count and sing a song. *It's time to draw and sing a song.*
Clap your hands, and now sit down! *Clap your hands, and now sit down!*

1

CHANT TR: 1.2 p.8

Stand up.
Sit down.
Touch your head.
Run around.
[Repeat two more times.]

Chant and Song Lyrics

CHANT TR: 2.2 p.16

It's cloudy. It's cloudy.
It's very, very cloudy.
It's cloudy. It's cloudy.
It's very, very cloudy.

It's windy. It's windy.
It's very, very windy.
It's windy. It's windy.
It's very, very windy.

Oh! It's raining. It's raining.
It's really, really raining.
Umbrella. Umbrella.
I need an umbrella!

SONG TR: 2.4 p.19
What's the Weather?

What's the weather?
What's the weather?
What's the weather like today?
Tell us, tell us.
What's the weather?
What's the weather like today?

Is it sunny?
Is it cloudy?
Is it windy out today?
Is it raining?
Is it snowing?
What's the weather like today?

Chant and Song Lyrics

3   **CHANT** TR: 3.2   p.24

A lion, a lion,
A big, brown lion.
Run, run, lion.

A frog, a frog,
A small, green frog.
Jump, jump, frog.

An elephant, an elephant,
A big, gray elephant.
Stomp, stomp elephant.

3   **SONG** TR: 3.4   p.27
What Is this Animal?

Can you guess?
What is this animal?
It has a big long nose and
two big teeth.
Big ears, big eyes, and
four big feet.
It is an elephant!

Can you guess?
What is this animal?
It has a small black nose and
big white face.
Black ears, black eyes, and
four black legs.
It is a panda!

Chant and Song Lyrics

4

CHANT TR: 4.2 p.32

I like singing.
[Sing la, la, la, la.]
I like dancing.
[Stomp your feet four times.]
I like clapping.
[Clap your hands four times.]
Singing
[Sing *la, la, la.*]
Dancing
[Stomp your feet three times.]
Clapping
[Clap your hands three times.]
Singing, dancing, clapping!

4

SONG TR: 4.4 p.35
Sing a Song

Sing a song, and beat on a drum.
Dance around, and stomp on
the ground.
Sing a song, and beat on a drum.
Dance around, and stomp on
the ground.

(Refrain)
Sing as loud as you can.
Sing along with a friend.
Sing a song, and beat on a drum.
Sing as loud as you can.
Sing along with a friend.
Sing a song, and beat on a drum.

Sing a song, and beat on a drum.
Clap your hands, and stomp on
the ground.
Sing a song, and beat on a drum.
Clap your hands, and stomp on
the ground.
(Refrain)

Chant and Song Lyrics

5 CHANT TR: 5.2 p.42

See. See. What do you see?
I see a bird,
and I see a tree.

Smell. Smell. What do you smell?
I smell rice
and beans, as well.

Hear. Hear. What do you hear?
I hear a piano
with my ears.

5 SONG TR: 5.4 p.45

Oh, What Do You See?

Oh, what do you see?
Oh, what do you see?
I see a penguin looking at me.

Oh, what do you hear?
Oh, what do you hear?
I hear a lion roaring in my ear.
Oh, where are you now?
Oh, where are you now?
I'm in a zoo with lots of animals.

Oh, what do you see?
Oh, what do you see?
I see a monkey looking at me.

Oh, what do you hear?
Oh, what do you hear?
I hear a tiger growling in my ear.
Oh, where are you now?
Oh, where are you now?
I'm in a zoo with lots of animals.

Chant and Song Lyrics

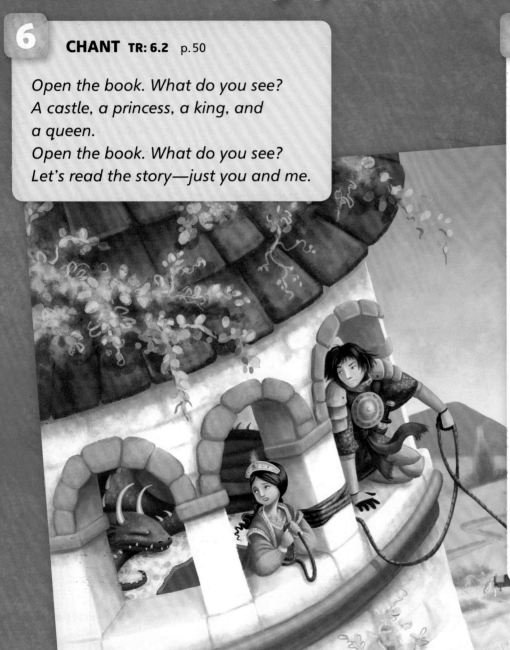

6   **CHANT** TR: **6.2**   p.50

Open the book. What do you see?
A castle, a princess, a king, and
a queen.
Open the book. What do you see?
Let's read the story—just you and me.

6   **SONG** TR: **6.4**   p.53
In a Castle

[Repeat each line.]
There is a princess in a castle.
Pretty, pretty princess.
A scary dragon, scary dragon
put her in his castle.
A knight climbs up so quietly,
to the castle window.
The scary dragon, scary dragon
is sleeping in his castle.
The pretty princess and the knight
climb out the castle window.
The scary dragon, scary dragon
is sleeping in his castle.
The pretty princess and the knight
are riding on a horse.
The scary dragon, scary dragon
is sleeping in his castle.
The pretty princess and the knight
are now the queen and king.
That's the end, that's the end of
our little story.

Chant and Song Lyrics

CHANT TR: 7.2 p.58

I see candles. I see cake.
Can I have some?
This tastes great!

I want candy. I want cake.
More please, more please.
Can I take?

I like candy. I like cake.
Uh-oh. I have a bellyache.

SONG TR: 7.4 p.61

It's a Party

[Repeat two times]
It's a party! It's a party!
We will have ice cream and candy!
There are lots of big balloons.
They are yellow, red, and blue!
Dance around! Dance around!
It's a party! It's a party!

It's a party! It's a party!
We will have a cake with candles!
There are lots of big balloons.
They are yellow, red, and blue!
Dance around! Dance around!
It's a party! It's a party!

Chant and Song Lyrics

8 **CHANT** TR: 8.2 p. 66

The cloud is white. The sky is blue.
The grass is green, and the trees are, too.
The cloud is white. The ocean is blue.
The grass is green, and the trees are, too.
We love our world, oh yes we do!
We love our world, oh yes we do!

8 **SONG** TR: 8.4 p. 69
Where Are You Going, Friend?

Hey, little, little rabbit!
Where are you going, friend?
Hopping, hopping all around.
Where do you live, friend?
I live in the mountain!

Hey, little, little fish!
Where are you going, friend?
Swimming, swimming all around.
Where do you live, friend?
I live in the ocean!

Hey, little, little bird!
Where are you going, friend?
Flying, flying all around.
Where do you live, friend?
I live in the clouds and sky!

CREDITS

NATIONAL GEOGRAPHIC
LEARNING

National Geographic Learning,
a Cengage Company

Welcome to Our World 3 Student's Book
Second Edition

Series Editors: Joan Kang Shin, JoAnn (Jodi) Crandall

Authors: Jill Korey O'Sullivan, Joan Kang Shin

Publisher: Sherrise Roehr

Executive Editor: Eugenia Corbo

Senior Development Editor: Mary Whittemore

Director of Global Marketing: Ian Martin

Heads of Regional Marketing:

    Charlotte Ellis (Europe, Middle East and Africa)

    Justin Kaley (Asia)

    Irina Pereyra (Latin America)

Senior Product Marketing Manager: David Spain

Content Project Manager: Ruth Moore

Media Researcher: Rebecca Ray

Art Director: Brenda Carmichael

Operations Support: Avi Mednick

Manufacturing Planner: Mary Beth Hennebury

Composition: Symmetry Creative Productions, Inc.

For permission to use material from this text or product,
submit all requests online at **cengage.com/permissions**
Further permissions questions can be emailed to
permissionrequest@cengage.com

Welcome to Our World 3 Student's Book Second Edition
ISBN: 978-0-357-50735-3

**Welcome to Our World 3 Student's Book with Online Practice
and Student's eBook**
Second Edition
ISBN: 978-0-357-63822-4

National Geographic Learning
200 Pier 4 Boulevard
Boston, MA 02210
USA

Locate your local office at **international.cengage.com/region**

Visit National Geographic Learning online at **ELTNGL.com**
Visit our corporate website at **www.cengage.com**

Printed in Mexico
Print Number: 02 Print Year: 2022